FINISHING LINE PRESS
www.finishinglinepress.com

CRAYON COLORS FOR SERIAL KILLERS

poems by

Sue William Silverman

Finishing Line Press
Georgetown, Kentucky

CRAYON COLORS FOR SERIAL KILLERS

For
Marc J. Sheehan, with love, always

Because

Ellen Lesser inspired this collection with a writing prompt during the Postgraduate Writers' Conference, Vermont College of Fine Arts, August, 2020.

The Year 2020 informed this collection through the wrath of the pandemic and the fury of political and civil unrest.

ISBN 978-1-64662-871-1 First Edition

Also by Sue William Silverman

Poetry

Hieroglyphics in Neon
If the Girl Never Learns

Creative Nonfiction

How to Survive Death and Other Inconveniences
The Pat Boone Fan Club: My Life as a White Anglo-Saxon Jew
Love Sick: One Woman's Journey through Sexual Addiction
Because I Remember Terror, Father, I Remember You
(winner: Association of Writers and Writing Programs Award Series)

Craft

Fearless Confessions: A Writer's Guide to Memoir

Publisher: Leah Huete de Maines
Editor: Christen Kincaid
Cover Art: Marc J. Sheehan
Author Photo: Jess Dewes
Cover Design: Elizabeth Maines McCleavy

Order online: www.finishinglinepress.com
also available on amazon.com

Author inquiries and mail orders:
Finishing Line Press
PO Box 1626
Georgetown, Kentucky 40324
USA

Table of Contents

I’m competent, sane, and I’m trying to tell the truth.
Aileen Wuornos

HER PALETTE

Eat heart, soul, you sky-
eyed girl, ghost face unmasked glass
façade of cracked moon.

Maskless mouths, droplets
shearing tar roof, slanting to
blue-limbo silence.

Burned moons, frigid suns
red aquatic equator
tilting ice-scorched soul.

Empty windows, streets
strewn yellow plague dust gust, sheets
billow wilting limbs.

Sighs cloaked *noir* disease
slashed veins, viral moths plaguing
streets of haloed hair.

Locked in damp concrete
swallowing steel, spine rigid,
chartreuse cypress cough.

Neon damp bar, you
slithering off stool after
his lazy heart stopped.

Pavement puddled gray
reflecting miraged soul—light
extinguished a prayer.

Masked eyes, drawn shades—blood
shot nameless heart beating on
lost smutty mattress.

Fevered seduction
pupil dyed iris acid—
hatching lusty death.

Raw tonsils, larynx,
pseudomembrane green toxic
scents inflamed longing.

Inhale bronze twilight
exhale leaden dawn-drenched song
noteless and bereft.

STORY TIME

The Serial Killer Prepares for Her High School Reunion

She zips a slash of red taffeta, slips on satin spikes. A riot of curls. She arranges her face listening to crime segments on the local news. She lives alone in a penthouse, overlooking the skyline, decorated, however, as if she stumbled into an Edward Hopper. Venetian blinds cast shadows across inherited Oriental rugs. She sleeps on silky sheets dreaming dreams she no longer remembers yet can't forget. She wears a platinum cross close to her thrumming heart. She sprays gardenia scent on cool white wrists her boyfriend once kissed before he vanished.

At the Serial Killer's Convention

Her packed valise weights her hotel bed. She unwraps her masks—now conveniently mandatory during the pandemic. Behind them she is dream-girl; matron; high school slut. She cruises vendor tables seeking capes the color of shadows, vials of invisible ink, unguents for oblivion. She will return home the same way she got here—claim an entrance ramp, stick out her traffic-stopping thumb, and smile.

The Serial Killer in Quarantine

Researchers in West Virginia discover zombie cicadas under the influence of a mind-controlling fungus, unknowingly infecting others. She eyes the clueless young man who delivers groceries to her door. She settles in for a solitary dinner then a game of solitaire with Tarot cards to see if she can best her fate.

The Serial Killer as a Young Girl on First Day of School

She climbs the bus stairs, settles beside a boy with blonde hair. In her backpack are sharpened pencils, fresh crayons, and brightly colored safety scissors designed for little hands to manipulate and not get fatigued.

The Serial Killer Prepares for the Holidays

She balances swan feathers on pine needles, mimicking snow, or flight, or falling. Holiday lights shine but do not disco or gyrate unless a visitor's head should spin. She bakes gingerbread men, arranges them on a festive platter, drapes a linen napkin on her lap, and eats.

The Serial Killer Celebrates Independence Day

The Fourth of July dawns pink and bright. She slips into her yellow bikini. She packs a picnic lunch of egg salad sandwiches and Fritos, nestles Coke in the cooler, and tucks a towel under her arm. She arranges herself just above the wrack of seaweed littering the sand. She slips on a straw hat and slathers Coppertone on her pale shoulders. Through the lenses of her tinted X-ray specs, she watches revelers play Frisbee, sunbathe, and dip their dark bones in timid waves.

The Serial Killer Searches for Answers

She scrolls Ancestry.com as if hearing faint echoes from a balalaika, a Celtic tune, a symphony of French horns, clavichords. All the strings on a harp spiral into DNA helixes of lost interstates, cul-de-sacs, exits leading nowhere. She seeks company but only finds shadows of herself.

The Serial Killer Visits the Flea Market

Broken record players, radios missing dials, ripped t-shirts, rings absent glass gems, sandals with frayed straps. Is she the only one who knows why nothing lasts?

The Serial Killer's Night Out at a Bar

As if location were time, she sits on a stool in a position of quarter past midnight. She wears couture, Balmain. The bartender mixes her daiquiri from Bacardi and demerara syrup. His delicate fingers squeeze lime, a quick grate of rind. She already tastes the dark edge that lasts till morning.

HER SUBJECTS

Feathers crisp, mildewed
beaks, stopped air silent, café
coffee, shuttered dawn.

Concave stomach, slate
eyes, rain coursing gutters, frayed
words, fractured features.

Sealed eyelids, lashes
anemic as lust or love
palliative death.

Nests fall, eggs crack off-
key silence, puncture ear drums
throb hollow sorrow.

Lost brick alleys lost
riptides lost throats dusky thrush
lost cells fungal, hot.

Distorted ribs breathe
failing stars, rhomboid sight ice
slicked iris, shut now.

Consonants cracking
freckles metastasizing
envelopes empty.

Disturbed piano
keys crack earth disfigure pine
barrens—mythic loss.

Frosted fingers sprout
pine straw like spring daffodils
summer melt grave, moist.

Diphtheria blood,
tetanus cultures invade
petri dishes, throats.

Empty as sorrow
rivers floating lost dirge boats
no destination.

Sue William Silverman is an award-winning author of seven books of creative nonfiction and poetry. Her most recent book, *How to Survive Death and Other Inconveniences*, won the Gold Star in Foreword Reviews INDIE Book of the Year Award. It also won the 2021 Clara Johnson Award for Women's Literature sponsored by The Jane's Story Press Foundation.

Her first book, *Because I Remember Terror, Father, I Remember You*, won the Association of Writers and Writing Programs award in creative nonfiction. Her other nonfiction books include *Love Sick: One Woman's Journey through Sexual Addiction*, also made into a Lifetime TV original movie; *The Pat Boone Fan Club: My Life as a White Anglo-Saxon Jew*; and *Fearless Confessions: A Writer's Guide to Memoir.* Individual essays have won contests with *Water~Stone Review, Hotel Amerika, Mid-American Review, Blue Mesa Review, Under the Sun*, and the *Los Angeles Review.*

Her poetry collection, *If the Girl Never Learns*, won two gold awards from the Human Relations Indie Book Award Series. An earlier poetry collection is *Hieroglyphics in Neon.*

As a professional speaker, Sue has given readings, workshops, and presentations at scores of colleges and non-profit organizations. Her media interviews include *The View, Anderson Cooper–360*, and *PBS-Books*. She teaches in the MFA in Writing program at Vermont College of Fine Arts.

Please visit www.SueWilliamSilverman.com for more information, and follow her on Twitter @SueSilverman; on Instagram at suewilliamsilverman, or on Facebook, SueWilliamSilverman.

www.ingramcontent.com/pod-product-compliance
Lightning Source LLC
LaVergne TN
LVHW041600070426
835507LV00011B/1207